Really Short Walks
North Cornwall

Paul White

Bossiney Books · Launceston

This reprint 2010
First published 2008 by
Bossiney Books Ltd, Langore, Launceston, Cornwall PL15 8LD
www.bossineybooks.com
© 2008 Paul White   All rights reserved
ISBN 978-1-906474-07-2

Acknowledgements
The maps are by Graham Hallowell. Cover based on a design by
Heards Design Partnership. Photographs by the author
Printed in Great Britain by R Booth Ltd, Penryn, Cornwall

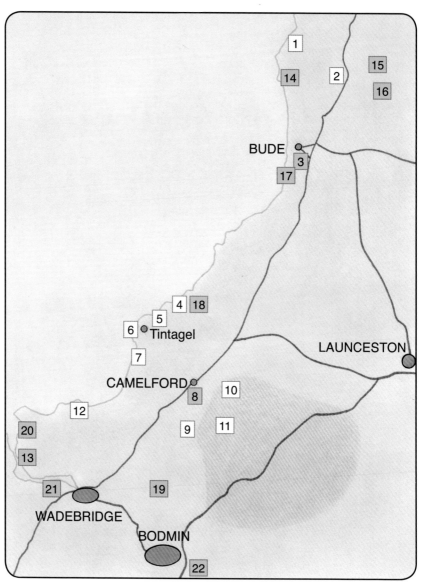

*The approximate locations of the walks in this book –
easier walks are indicated by green squares*

All the walks in this book were checked prior to printing, at which time
the instructions were correct. However, changes can occur in the
countryside over which neither the author nor the publisher has any
control. Please let us know if you encounter any serious problems.

Introduction

The delightful walks in this book are mostly 3-5km (2-3 miles) in length. Some are easy, others short but challenging. All have been chosen to show the wonderful scenic variety of north Cornwall – cliffs and beaches, woodland and moorland. We have not suggested how long they will take, because readers' walking abilities will vary considerably, nor have we selected the walks with pushchairs or wheelchairs in mind: most would be unsuitable on this inevitably rugged terrain.

Clothing and footwear

Do go prepared. Cornish weather can change rapidly, and even within a short walk there may be a considerable temperature difference when you climb from a sheltered valley to a cliff top exposed to an Atlantic breeze. Always carry extra layers of clothing as well as a waterproof. On most paths, especially inland, you are likely to come across briars, thorns and nettles, so bare legs are a liability.

There will be some mud at most times of the year and perhaps a lot of mud and puddles in winter and after a wet spell. Ideally, therefore, wear walking boots – and certainly not sandals! Walking any distance in wellington boots is not recommended, as they don't provide ankle support, but a single short walk of under 5km shouldn't cause a problem for most people. Just watch out for uneven ground, especially on the cliff path. I find a walking pole is a considerable help. It is sensible to carry water with you, as dehydration causes tiredness.

Safety

Be careful when walking the cliff path because it is not fenced off from the drop. Go no nearer the edge than you have to: you might be standing on an overhang. Take special care when the path does take you near the edge, and keep a close eye on children and dogs.

The sketch maps in this book are just that – sketches. You may want to carry an OS 1:25,000 map for extra information, and certainly it is advisable to have sheet 109 to hand if you venture on Bodmin Moor.

The Cornish countryside

Despite many pressures on their livelihoods, Cornish farmers are still trying to make a living from the land you will pass through. Please respect their crops. Leave gates closed or open as you find them, and keep dogs under control, especially during the lambing season.

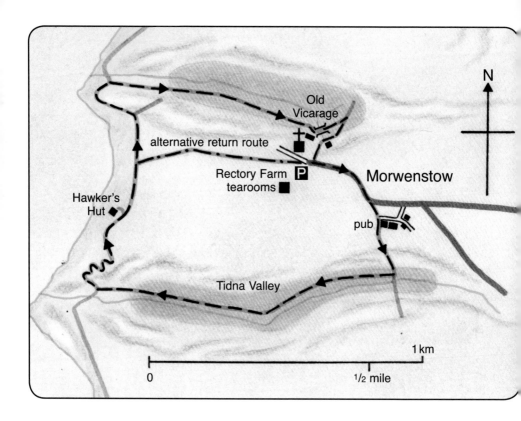

Walk 1 Morwenstow

Distance: 3.4km (2 miles)

Character: A short walk, but strenuous, including one steep and one very, very steep ascent. A dramatic coastline (saw-toothed rocks below, just waiting for wrecks, and open fields on the clifftops) is intermixed with delightful wooded valleys and burbling brooks – and paths likely to be muddy after rain.

Start from Morwenstow Church. Walk back inland along the lane to the village green and head across to the Bush Inn. A footpath runs immediately to the right of the inn, then cuts diagonally across the beer garden to a stile in the far left corner. Descend to another stile which leads into the wooded Tidna Valley. At the foot, keep right along the valley bottom, signed to the COASTPATH.

When you reach the coast path, turn right. The path is seriously steep, with steps and zig-zags. Once you are near the top, you will see on the left a path down to Hawker's Hut, at 100m altitude surely

4

Britain's highest beach hut. Shortly beyond this you will reach a wooden gate, and here you have a choice.

If you are short of time or energy, or if you are concerned about the totally unfenced cliff edge ahead, and a fairly vertiginous descent, you may wish to turn right immediately after the gate, and follow the path straight back to the church.

Otherwise, continue ahead on the coast path as signed. Follow the coast path left (acorn sign) and down, keeping children and dogs under close control. Near the foot, turn right (white arrow waymark) and follow the path up the sheltered valley.

Cross a footbridge just below the Old Vicarage. At a path junction turn sharp right, up through the Old Vicarage gardens (please keep quiet and stick to the path) and into the churchyard. Climb the path which has a metal handrail, up to the gate, which leads out to the car park. The Rectory Tearooms are heartily recommended, and the Bush Inn is also very close.

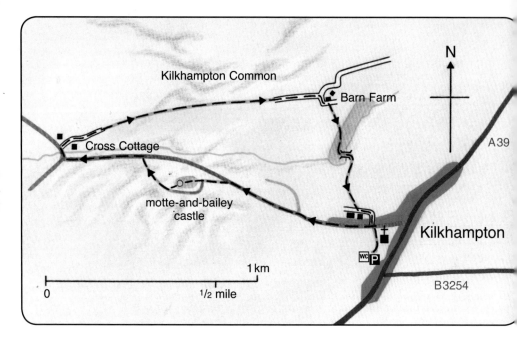

Walk 2 Kilkhampton

Distance: 4.1 km (2 1/2 miles)
*Character: An inland walk mainly on footpaths and some quiet lanes,
with woodland, open fields and a stretch of ancient trackway – and
also the earthworks of a twelfth century motte-and-bailey castle (see
the top photograph opposite).*

Start from the car park beside Kilkhampton Church. Walk through
the churchyard, to the left of the church. Turn left along the lane
and continue for about 850 m (half a mile) till you reach a PUBLIC
FOOTPATH bearing off to the left, which will lead you to a motte-and-
bailey castle.

A gate gives access to the earthworks, which are small scale but very
well preserved. Go through the gate at the far end of the earthworks to
rejoin the footpath. Keep right, downhill. The path circles back to the
lane. Turn left. After 400 m, turn right at a road junction (WOODBURY),
then at 'Cross Cottage' turn right (PUBLIC FOOTPATH).

A stony track leads up to Kilkhampton Common, where no common
land appears to survive. This track is probably an ancient drove road
providing access through enclosed fields to common grazing on the
higher ground. In Spring its hedges are full of flowers.

6

When you reach Barn Farm, turn right on the concrete drive around the outside, then take the waymarked footpath through a field gate towards the church. A stile gives access to a footpath which leads down through a bluebell wood. Cross a stream at the bottom, and climb fairly steeply up the footpath on the other side.

A ladder stile at the top gives access to a track. Turn left, then follow the track round to the right and up to a lane. Cross straight over and retrace your steps through the churchyard.

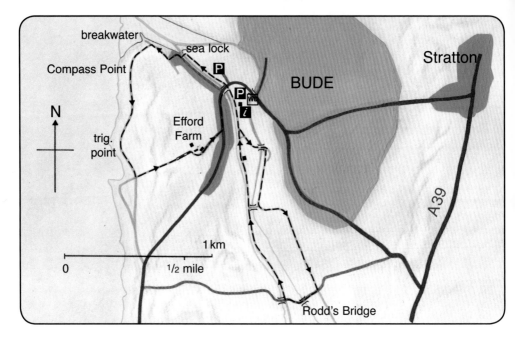

Walk 3   A Bude figure of eight walk

Distance: Two loops, each 3km (2 miles)
Character: Two contrasting walks which can be done together or
separately. The coastal loop includes the lock, the breakwater and some
lovely coastal scenery, with one modest ascent. The inland loop is
well-surfaced and entirely flat (even suitable for a wheelchair) and
includes the canal towpath as well as an opportunity for bird-watching
in Bude Marsh.

Both walks start on the towpath beside the Bude Visitor Centre.

For the coastal loop: facing the canal, turn right. Cross the road and
continue towards the sea with the canal on your left. On your right
you will pass the Castle, which is actually a house built in 1830, now
home to the Bude museum and a restaurant.

   Cross the canal by the lock gates and turn right, then almost immediately left up a short flight of steps, and right again past East Cottage.
At another flight of steps, turn right, COAST PATH. At a waymark, the
coast path turns off left, but you may well want to continue down to
the breakwater. (Do not venture out on it if the sea is rough.)

   Return to the waymark and turn right up the cliff on the coast path
(noticing the compass on the stone shelter at Compass Point).

At the very top of the slope you'll pass a trig. point (a concrete pillar from which, in the past, map surveyors took their readings). Descend to the next gate. Don't go through, but turn left, unsigned, along the wall. At the field corner, continue ahead through the kissing gate, and at the end of the next field go through a gate and down a track.

Pass a pond and immediately turn right over a stile. Take the access drive to the right of the buildings, and walk down to the main road. Turn left and you will soon reach the bridge over the canal.

For the inland loop: facing the canal, turn left. When there's a choice of path, fork left on the CYCLE PATH. Cross a bridge and immediately turn right off the tarmac – unless you have a pushchair or wheelchair, in which case follow the cycle path which loops around – and after 100m rejoin the cycle path.

Pass a rugby ground and turn left, HELE BRIDGE. After another 700m you will reach a lane. Turn right along it, cross the river and when you reach the canal turn right along the towpath. Now walk with the canal on your left back to the starting point, passing a bird hide on the way.

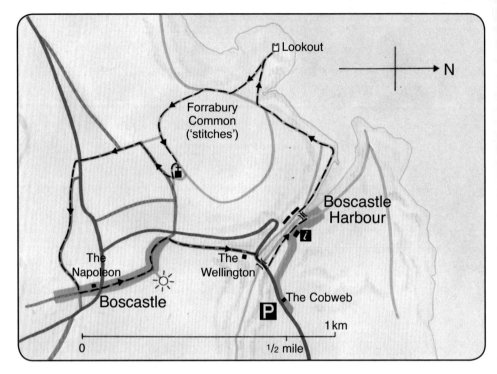

Walk 4 Boscastle

Distance: 4km (2¹/₂ miles)
Character: Few walks can include quite as many points of interest in
so short a distance. Apart from the attractions of the harbour itself,
there is some stunning cliff scenery, an Iron Age promontory fort, a
rare example of medieval strip farming on Forrabury Common, the
picturesque medieval main street of Boscastle village and the mound
on which stood the Norman castle which gave the village its name.

There is one fairly steep ascent, and the coastal paths are uneven
and sometimes slippery, so take care. A much more detailed
commentary on this walk can be found in Jim Castling's book What to
see in Boscastle, *on sale in the village.*

Start from the main Boscastle car park and head down towards the
harbour. Bear right into a cobbled alleyway beside the Old Oil House.
This runs parallel to the riverside path, then joins it. Pass the Boscastle
Visitor Centre, turn left across the bridge, then right along the quay
wall. (If you want to avoid the steepest part of the ascent, bear left on
a path with a yellow waymark: this is more gently graded.) Otherwise

continue to the pier, climb the steps and keep left up the rocky path. It's a long ascent, but if you stop every twenty paces or so to look back at the extraordinary view, no one will blame you!

Turn right when you reach WILLA PARK, cross the ancient defences and climb to the Lookout, now used by the Coastwatch. As you return, take the right fork in the path. Ahead of you on Forrabury Common lies a medieval open field system – individually leased strips known as 'stitches'. Turn right along the coast path, then fork left around the stitches to the church.

Turn right into and through the churchyard. Facing inland, bear right past an old Celtic cross. Turn right along the lane, which, after 200 m, turns left. Follow it to the main Boscastle-Tintagel road. Cross directly over, and turn left along the path.

Continue ahead along Paradise Road. At a crossroads turn left down High Street, past the Napoleon Inn. Cross over and continue down Fore Street, past more ancient cottages.

As the street curves left, a short unmarked path to the right leads up to the motte on which 'Bottreaux Castle' once stood – worth a diversion. Continue down the street, and shortly after Pillar House keep right downhill. (Stay alert for cars coming down behind you.) Pass the Wellington Hotel, then turn right across the main road bridge and back to the car park.

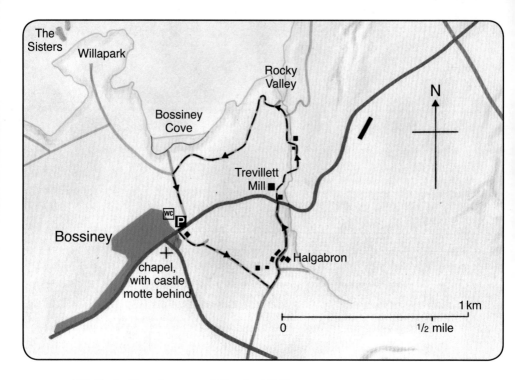

Walk 5   Bossiney and Rocky Valley

Distance: 3km (2 miles)
*Character: Starting quietly through farmland, this gradually develops
into one of the most dramatic walks in Cornwall. It is quite strenuous,
involving descents and ascents – one of which is very steep – as well
as some uneven walking, and rocks which are slippery especially when
wet. If you want to impress some lively children with the beauties of
the Cornish coast even when the tide is covering their favourite beach,
this walk is ideal, but it's not one for the frail or unsteady.*

Start from the parking area at the north-east end of Bossiney village,
near a transmitter mast. This is the parking space for Bossiney Cove
and beach, and public toilets are provided here. (If this area is full, you
could park opposite the entrance to Trevillett Mill.)

Start by walking into Bossiney, towards Tintagel. After 60 metres or
so, turn left on PUBLIC FOOTPATH and descend the track with mobile
homes on your left, then turn right across the stream. Cross a field to
a gateway, then another field to a stile, and a third field to a gateway
with a yellow disc on a pole (at the time of writing).

Turn left along the lane, through the hamlet of Halgabron, and down to the Tintagel-Boscastle road. Cross straight over, into the grounds of Trevillett Mill. Follow the footpath signs and cross the stream by a footbridge. Where the path re-crosses the stream, you will pass through the ruins of Trewethet Mill, just behind which are the famous Rocky Valley carvings.

Continue with the stream now on your right. Ignore the next footbridge. A few metres further on, you may wish to divert briefly to the right to see where the stream meets the sea – but do take care. Then climb the steep steps to the summit, where the views are stunning. From this point the coast path becomes a little more sedate, winding its way along the cliff past old farming terraces, then heading inland.

When you reach a short flight of steps down to an old holloway (a deep track), you have a choice. You could turn right down the holloway to the cove with its sandy beach, or continue further along the coast path to Willapark or even to Tintagel. Or you could simply turn left up the holloway, and make your way up the slope to the start, by the transmitter mast.

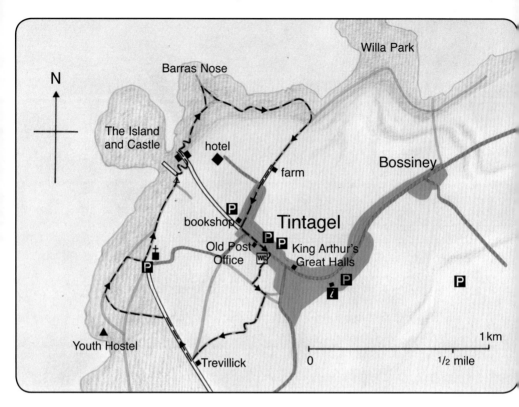

Walk 6   Tintagel

Distance: 5km (3 miles)

Character: Stunning views of the coast and of the heart of Arthurian Tintagel – the Castle. There is steep and uneven walking on the cliff path in places, and slate surfaces can be slippery so take care.

The walk starts from the Old Post Office in the centre of Tintagel. Head up the street and after 100m turn right, FOOTPATH TO CHURCH. Walk through a car park, then down and across a stream. Turn left, TRERAMMETT, and at the next path junction turn right, TREVILLICK.

Keep the wall on your right, cross two stiles then in the third field turn right across a stile into a confined path which leads into another field. When the path divides, keep left up the slope. At the top, turn right along a track towards the church (signed TO THE COASTPATH). After 200m, turn left, YOUTH HOSTEL. Continue out to the coast path and turn right along it. You will get your first sight of the Island, with its vertical cliff confronting the Atlantic.

14

You may well want to divert to the church, dedicated to St Materiana, which almost certainly occupies a pre-Christian sacred site. The building itself is mainly Norman, and contains a Roman carved 'milestone'. From the church car park (an alternative starting point for the walk) take the well-surfaced path near the churchyard wall.

Descend some rough steps, then turn left, either athletically across a stile or – 10m further on and much more sedately – through a gateway. At the castle entrance, turn right and zigzag down past the toilets, seasonal café and English Heritage shop. Turn right across the stream, and right again up steps. (To the left is an area which once housed winches and derricks used to load slate into coasting vessels.)

Follow the COAST PATH upward. When it levels out, look back for a view of the platforms on which the castle buildings – and perhaps their sixth century predecessors – were constructed. At a path junction, bear left out to Barras Nose for the views, then as you return, keep left along a grassy path back to the coast path, turning left for BOSSINEY.

On reaching a waymarked junction, turn right up the slope, keep left through a gate and cross a field keeping the wall on your left. Another gate leads to a track, then to a street.

Continue ahead, turning left by the King Arthur Bookshop, and you will arrive back at the Old Post Office.

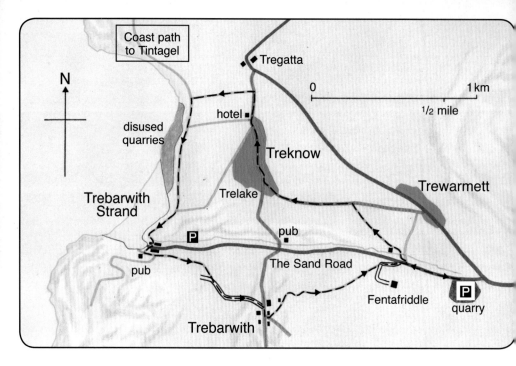

Walk 7 Trebarwith

Distance: 5.6km (3¹/₂ miles)
Character: A fairly strenuous walk, with two steep ascents, one very steep descent and some uneven surfaces. It provides a variety of scenery, from farmland and woodland to cliff views of coast and beach.

Park in the free quarry car park at the top of the road down to Trebarwith Strand ('the Sand Road'). Turn left out of the car park and walk down the road for 300m, then turn right, PUBLIC FOOTPATH.

At the foot of the steps, do not cross the wooden footbridge. Turn left across the stile, then over the stone clapper bridge. Walk carefully through the grounds of a house, following the signs, then up through a small wood and across a field to a lane.

Turn left along the lane, which soon bears right into the hamlets of Trelake and Treknow – with their older houses somewhat over-run by new development, but still very attractive. Keep right at junctions and follow the main street uphill to a bench-topped mound.

If you have a problem with high stiles, you may wish to take the track signed as a footpath past the front of the Penallick Hotel, but it can be very wet underfoot and you miss some interesting scenery.

Otherwise, continue past the Penallick Hotel for a further 100m, then turn left, TO THE COASTPATH. Either way, turn left when you reach the coast path. You will see the impressive remains of a series of slate quarries.

Before long you will arrive at a footpath junction: keep right and begin the seriously steep descent to Trebarwith Strand. At the road, you will find shops, cafés, public conveniences, and of course a fabulous beach. When ready to continue, cross the road and head up to the Port William pub, with its dramatic views as seen in the photo above, and turn left for THE COASTPATH.

After 80m, at a stile, leave the coast path and continue ahead up a rocky track, once the main access to the beach but now a footpath. Join a track which leads up to the hamlet of Trebarwith.

Reaching the road at Trebarwith Farm, turn right, then left (DELABOLE), then left again (PUBLIC FOOTPATH TREWARMETT). The waymarks were rather intermittent when I last walked it. Beside an old farm building, go straight ahead through a gate, then keep the wall on your right. At a pair of gateways, take the one on the left then keep the hedge on your right to another gateway. Bear 45° left across the next field to a stone stile. Continue in the same direction and a stile in the far left corner of the field leads into a farm driveway. Descend the drive to the road, and turn right back to the car park.

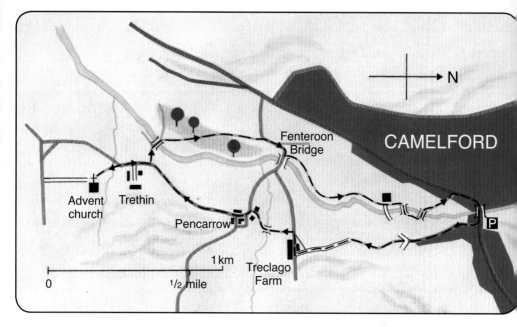

Walk 8 Camelford to Advent church

Distance: 4.7km (3 miles). Can be cut to 4km (2¹/₂ miles)
Character: An inland walk, outward along the east side of the River
Camel to the isolated church of St Adwena, then back along the other
bank. Varied scenery – farmland, woodland and riverbank.

Start from the car park beside the river bridge in Camelford. On leaving the car park, cross the main road into COLLEGE ROAD. The lane climbs gently. At the end, cross a stile into a field and descend by way of another stile to a footbridge. Climb the footpath on the other side, which crosses two fields before entering a track.

The track leads out to a lane at Treclago Farm. Turn right, and after 100m (just after a triangle of ground) turn left across a stile. Descend the field to cross a footbridge. Bear right up across the next field to a stile. A path leads from here to a lane. Turn left, then almost immediately follow the lane as it turns right, signed ADVENT CHURCH.

After 650m, just as the lane bends to the left, you will see a PUBLIC FOOTPATH on the right. You may wish to shorten the walk by turning right here now. Otherwise continue along the lane past Trethin, then take the PUBLIC FOOTPATH which bears off to the left, crosses a streamlet and then heads up to the church.

18

Retrace your steps past Trethin, and turn left on the PUBLIC FOOT-PATH down the slope. At the bottom, turn right along the river bank for a few metres to a footbridge. Cross, then bear diagonally right across the meadow. The path enters a bluebell wood and climbs through it, then heads across to a lane.

Turn right on the lane, down the hill. Immediately before Fenteroon Bridge, turn left on a PUBLIC FOOTPATH. This follows the bank with the river on your right, briefly crossing and recrossing the river as you enter the town.

You will suddenly emerge through an archway onto Camelford's busy main street – be very careful if you have children or dogs with you. The change from the tranquillity of the riverside to the roar of HGVs climbing a steep and narrow hill is quite dramatic.

Turn right down the main street. When the road swings to the right, cross over at the pedestrian lights, and turn right across the river bridge. The car park is on the left. Camelford offers all kinds of shops, pubs and restaurants, as well as the North Cornwall Museum and Gallery.

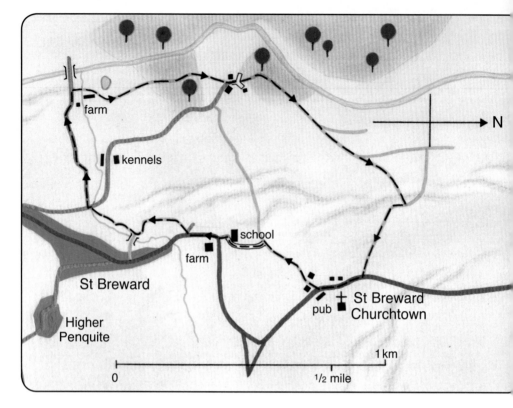

Walk 9   St Breward

Distance: 3.3km (2 miles)
Character: Much variety on a small scale and some distinctive
Bodmin Moor countryside – woodland, farmland, bleak moorland
scrub. This is a short but at times quite tricky walk. There is some
uneven walking, as well as difficult stiles and one long steady ascent.
St Breward historically was dependent on its granite quarries and
china clay extraction, and it still has the feeling of a working village,
criss-crossed by footpaths which must have been trudged daily by men,
women and children on their way to work.

Start from the church of St Breward (SX097774) and walk down to
the Old Inn. Turn right on a PUBLIC FOOTPATH, passing the front of
a house, crossing a farm access track, then entering a narrow walled
path. Where it becomes a track, keep left, ignoring the massive steps
of a stone stile. Pass the village school, then turn right joining the
main road for 100m.

Just before 'Mor-Ray', bear right on a PUBLIC FOOTPATH, which winds round and down to a footbridge. Don't cross the bridge but continue downhill with the stream on your left.

Reaching a tarmac track, turn left and immediately right down a lane. (We found some difficulties with the footpath shown on the OS map, and the lane is very quiet.)

At the foot of the hill, turn right (PUBLIC FOOTPATH). Cross the stream and walk past a large barn, then keep right of a pond and follow the signs. Continue ahead at a lane, then almost immediately ahead again on PUBLIC FOOTPATH.

Follow the main path as it bends right then heads steadily uphill, keeping right and uphill at several forks. When you meet a path cutting across at an oblique angle, turn right and continue uphill to the road. Turn right back to the church.

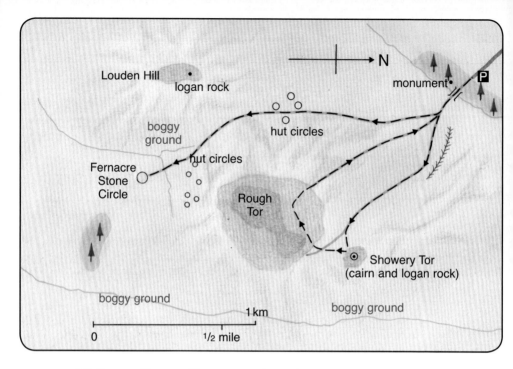

Walk 10   Two walks at Roughtor (or Rough Tor)

Distances: To the stone circle and back, 5km (3 miles)
To Showery Tor and Roughtor, about 3.25km (2 miles)
Character: Roughtor is one of the two dramatic granite outcrops which
dominate Bodmin Moor, and the area is popular with local walkers.
A wide variety of walks is possible from the large car park. We have
shown a couple of alternatives on the map – but there are many paths,
human and animal, and it is impossible to give precise directions. The
area is one of great prehistoric interest, with many visible remains.

Care needed: Although you will not be far from your car, this is open
moorland: low cloud sometimes envelops the tor. If you have children,
they will probably enjoy scrambling on the granite boulders of
Roughtor, with obvious risks. Boggy ground is best avoided, especially
after a wet spell. Although the path to the stone circle crosses a stream,
it is generally passable if sometimes squelchy.

For the stone circle walk: Cross the stream heading towards Roughtor,
then after 100m bear right, picking up one of the paths heading just
to the right of and below the outcrop. Continue in the same direction
and cross over a stream, and you *should* see the circle ahead of you!

Up to Showery Tor and Roughtor: Cross the stream and head towards Roughtor, the largest of the three outcrops, then bear left on a path leading to the smallest outcrop, which is Showery Tor. From here, cross over to the main outcrop, and explore it as best suits your party!

Some of the features

Fernacre Stone Circle (photograph above) is probably about 4000-4500 years old. It is 45 metres in diameter, with most of the stones around waist height – a prehistoric parish church compared to the cathedral of Stonehenge, but an altogether different experience. You will probably be alone here, able to go where you please and touch the stones, always with the dramatic background of Roughtor.

On your way to the circle, you will pass through an ancient field system, with the remains of Cornish hedges thousands of years old, some with gateways. There are also hut circles spread about, of various sizes and probably not all dwellings: farmers needed barns and outhouses then as now. (The sketch map does not pretend to accuracy concerning their exact locations!)

Showery Tor is a natural outcrop, but was clearly seen as special since a huge cairn was built up around the tor in Neolithic times. Running next to the path up to Showery Tor is a cairn 500 m long, which was the subject of a *Timeteam* televised dig, and was also shown to be Neolithic in date (4500-2200 BC).

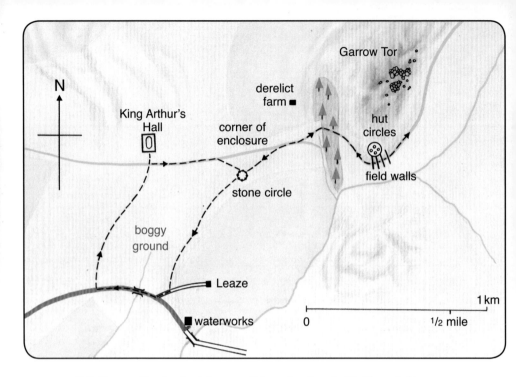

Walk 11 Bodmin Moor – King Arthur's Hall and Garrow

Distance: About 5km (3 miles) but can be shortened or extended
Character: A moorland walk, but with many features, so it's relatively
easy to navigate. Features include a stone circle, a Bronze Age
village, medieval fields and Cornwall's most enigmatic monument,
King Arthur's Hall. Map and compass desirable.

To get there: From the church at St Breward (6km or 4 miles south
of Camelford) head south towards the centre of the village, then bear
left (BODMIN). Go forward at a crossroads (BLISLAND) and at the next
junction turn left for BOLATHERICK and then keep right. After a
further 1.6km (1 mile) park at the roadside – shortly before a bridge
over a stream (SX128769).

Walk north towards Roughtor – a rocky hill beyond the near horizon –
keeping to the left of the boggy ground. You will soon see a fenced
enclosure, containing King Arthur's Hall. When you have explored
the site, head east. An old trackway with occasional guide stones runs
parallel on your right. Ahead lies the corner of a walled enclosure, and
just to the south of that lies a stone circle. It is one of a pair, but the
other lies on private land.

Head east-north-east to rejoin the trackway along the wall, and descend to a stile which gives access to a path through a long narrow belt of conifers. Another stile leads out of the wood. Bear right up the slope, and you will soon come to a Bronze Age farmstead which is worth exploring. Several well-preserved hut circles are surrounded by a stone wall.

Continue along the path for a few metres and you will find that it crosses the lines of several ancient field walls or 'reaves', heading down towards the river. Walk further along the path as far as you choose, and then retrace your steps to the stone circle.

Now keep the enclosure wall on your left and the boggy ground on your right as you head back to the lane. Turn right along the lane back to your car.

King Arthur's Hall, fancifully named, is a mysterious and unique structure of unknown origin and purpose. It looks prehistoric, but may be medieval. A bank surrounds a rectangular area 50 metres long. A row of upright stones lines the inside of the bank – presumably these are the backs of the knights' chairs!

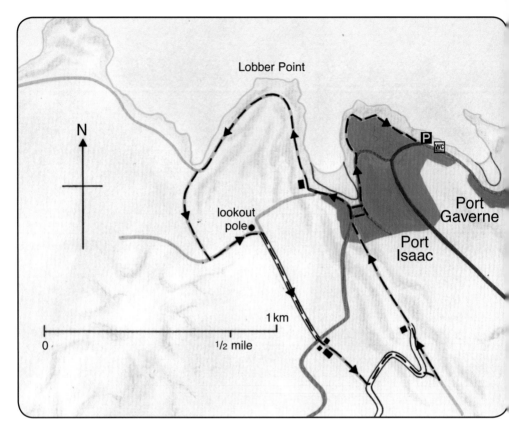

Walk 12 Port Isaac

Distance: 5km (3 miles)

Character: A lovely walk of great variety – a famously picturesque and televised fishing village, wind-blown cliffs with stunning views and two sheltered valleys. On the downside, there are two steep ascents, the valley bottom paths will be muddy after a wet spell, and you will pass a water treatment works. But it's well worth it!

Start from the main car park on the Port Gaverne side of Port Isaac. Descend to the lowest level and turn left along the path. Reaching the village, turn right downhill. Follow the road around the harbour and up ROSCARROCK HILL.

   Follow COAST PATH PUBLIC FOOTPATH PORT QUIN. Climb the steps up to the cliff top. Now follow the fairly level path around the headland and to the next cove.

26

Leave the coast path here, following a lesser path up the valley with the stream on your right for 500 m. At a path junction turn left, PORT ISAAC. Climb. At a yellow waymark continue ahead and pass the old lookout pole. At the top right corner of the field, turn right through a gate and along a walled track. This brings you to a lane.

Cross onto the PUBLIC FOOTPATH between 'North Light' and 'The Courtyard' and then to the left of an older building. Cross a stile and continue ahead. Keep the hedge on your right to another stile. Cross this and immediately turn left down a concrete track.

The track bends right. When it then turns a hairpin bend to the left, continue ahead on the waymarked footpath. Follow the path inland when it narrows. Just before a stile, turn sharp left on a well-beaten path along the valley bottom towards Port Isaac.

Turn right onto a drive then continue ahead on the footpath until you reach the village. Turn right down the road, take the first right, then first left at 'Leatside Cottage'. At the harbour turn right and retrace your steps to the car park.

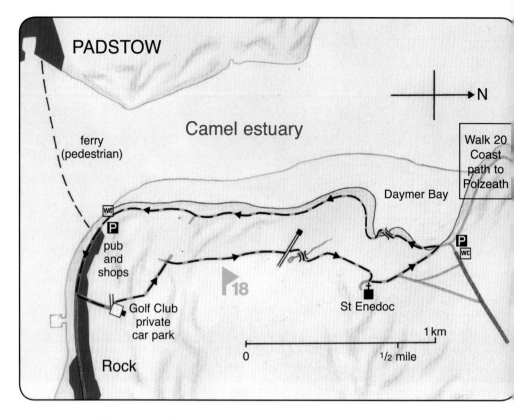

Walk 13   Rock and Daymer Bay

Distance: 4.5km (2³/4 miles)
Character: The outward leg is across a delightful links golf course, with distant views of the Camel estuary. The return is over and through dunes beside the sea. As well as a broad and easily accessible sandy beach, there is the tiny Norman church, St Enedoc's, famous for having once been all but swallowed up by the dunes, and for being the burial place of John Betjeman.

Start from the car park at Rock, near the ferry. (Alternatively start from Daymer Bay.) Walk back along the road past shops and the Rock Inn. Turn left up the lane which is signed to St Enedoc Golf Club.

Just before the club entrance, turn left on a tarmac track, then after 15m turn right into a narrow PUBLIC FOOTPATH. At a path junction, turn right to cross the golf course, following the instructions on the white notice board.

At a tarmac track, turn left then almost immediately right as signed, crossing a bridge then turning left. *NB Don't walk up the middle of the fairway!* You need to keep to the left of the fairway, then walk around the green at the far end, and swing back to visit the church, which is approached from its right side – see map.

On leaving the church, turn right along the obvious path, then at a junction bear left towards the sea and continue to a footpath junction almost at the beach. Unless you wish to visit the facilities at Daymer Bay (toilets, shop, etc) turn left along the coast path which runs parallel to the estuary, along the back of, then over and through the dunes.

At a bridge over a stream, continue uphill as signed, then, faced with a steep hill, turn right, and follow the path out to rejoin the old coast path. The dunes are a fragile environment, and walkers need to follow diversions of this kind to avoid eroding them further. The exact route through the dunes will consequently vary in detail, but will be roughly parallel to the beach.

Great flattish walks of North Cornwall

Walking in North Cornwall is not like strolling around Hyde Park. The hills and cliffs which give the landscape its grandeur make some of the routes in this book quite tough going.

We are therefore suggesting some further circular walks which are less dramatic but rather easier, as well as some enjoyable there-and-back walks. They fall into three main categories: disused railway lines, reservoirs, and river valleys leading inland from the coast. They are all simple to follow and will not even require a map.

14 Coombe Valley woods

An attractive woodland circuit of 2.5km (1½ miles). To get there, follow signs for COOMBE VALLEY from Kilkhampton, through Stibb. At the foot of the hill there is parking for half a dozen cars on the right.

Take the footpath from the parking area across the stream (see photo below), pass to the right of the mill and climb the bank. Then turn right along the forest track. After 1km, when the path divides, keep right across the stream, then right again to return along the opposite bank. The track begins to climb, but very gently, till it reaches a lane. Turn right down the lane for 350m back to the parking area.

Virworthy Wharf, on the Bude Aqueduct walk

15 Upper Tamar Lake

The Tamar Lakes lie east of Kilkhampton. A permissive path circles Upper Tamar Lake, which is used for fishing and sailing. The facilities include car park, toilets and seasonal café. The circuit is 5 km (3 miles) – just cross the dam and turn left around the lake. It can be muddy. Generally good for wildlife once away from the watersports centre.

16 Bude Aqueduct walk from Lower Tamar Lake

The Lower Lake is recommended for bird-watching and has a car park with toilets. Follow the signs for the Bude Aqueduct Walk. You can walk as far as you choose along the old Bude Canal. This branch of the canal started life simply as a water feed to the main canal, but it was later used to bring sand to Virworthy Wharf, returning with crops.

17 Widemouth Bay

Whilst not totally flat, the cliffs between Widemouth Bay and Bude are relatively level, certainly by the standards of the north Cornwall coast. Start from the free car park, just uphill from Widemouth Bay.

18 Boscastle and the Valency Valley
There is a delightful woodland walk following the Valency Valley inland from the main car park. Simply follow the valley upstream ignoring side paths.

19 Hellandbridge
The Camel Trail is primarily a cycle path, developed from a disused single-track mineral railway. South from Hellandbridge, where there is a free car park (SX065715), the trail runs through really attractive and varied woodland.

20 Polzeath to Daymer Bay
The coast path here involves a slight climb out of Polzeath, but then is fairly level all the way round to the car park at Daymer Bay. At that point it connects with Walk 13.

Two further flattish walks just out of area
21 The Camel Trail from Wadebridge to Padstow is a former railway line, now used as a cycle path and has pleasant views of the estuary. It is quite intensively used by cyclists, especially in season.

22 Cardinham Woods, just south of Bodmin (SX010667), has a car park from which a number of forest trails begin. The walks on either side of the river are virtually flat, and run through coniferous woodland. The side trails are often quite steep. There are toilets, a café, picnic facilities and children's play area.

Other Bossiney walks books you might find useful
Shortish Walks in north Cornwall (6-8km walks)
Shortish Walks – Bodmin Moor (6-8km walks)
Shortish Walks – St Ives to Padstow (6-8km walks)
Really short walks – North Dartmoor (3-5km walks)
Really short walks – South Dartmoor (3-5km walks)
Really short walks – North Devon (3-5km walks)